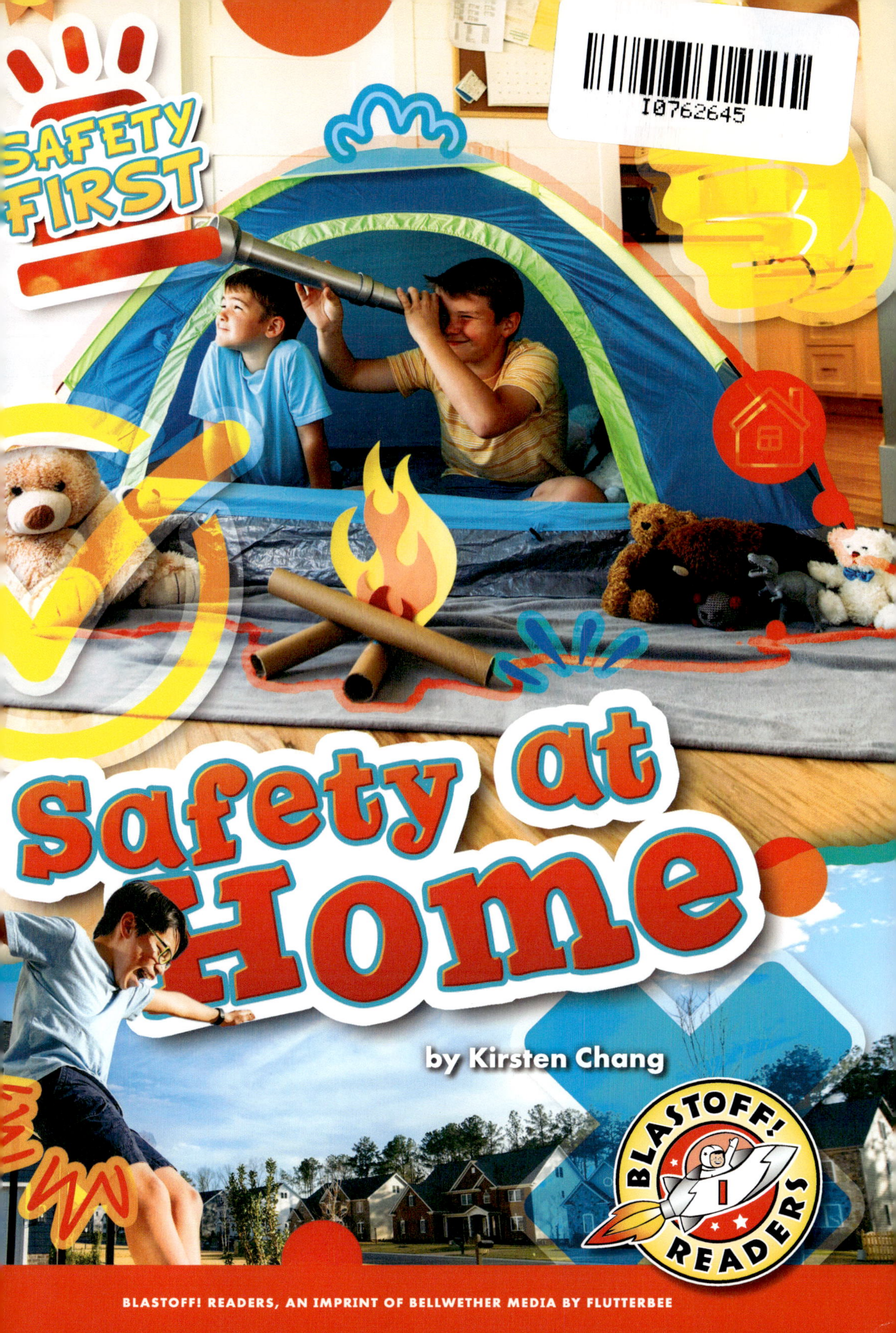

BLASTOFF! READERS, AN IMPRINT OF BELLWETHER MEDIA BY FLUTTERBEE

Blastoff! Readers are carefully developed by literacy experts to build reading stamina and move students toward fluency by combining standards-based content with developmentally appropriate text.

Level 1 provides the most support through repetition of high-frequency words, light text, predictable sentence patterns, and strong visual support.

Level 2 offers early readers a bit more challenge through varied sentences, increased text load, and text-supportive special features.

Level 3 advances early-fluent readers toward fluency through increased text load, less reliance on photos, advancing concepts, longer sentences, and more complex special features.

★ **Blastoff! Universe**

Reading Level

Grade K

Grades 1–3

Grade 4

This edition first published in 2027 by Bellwether Media, Inc.

For information regarding permission, write to Bellwether Media, Inc., Attention: Permissions Department, 3500 American Blvd W, Suite 150, Bloomington, MN 55431.

Library of Congress Cataloging-in-Publication Data is available at www.loc.gov or upon request from the publisher.

ISBN: 9798898800338 (hardcover)
ISBN: 9798898802868 (paperback)
ISBN: 9798898801571 (ebook)

Editor: Rachael Barnes Designer: Andrea Schneider

Printed in the United States of America, North Mankato, MN.

Table of Contents

Safety Starts at Home

Mira is careful around the hot oven. She bakes cookies with Dad. Time for sweet treats!

Why Stay Safe?

Home should be a safe place. But there are some **risks**.

Some items could hurt us if we touch or eat them.

Accidents can happen at home. It helps to be **prepared**.

FIRST AID

Staying Safe

Molly picks up her toys. Her baby brother could swallow little pieces.

Jonah helps in the kitchen. The stovetop is hot. He does not touch it.

Ava hears the **smoke alarm**. She follows the family plan for fires.

How to Practice Fire Safety

- **Know the number** to call if there is a fire.
- **Practice a fire escape plan** with your family.
- **Have a safe spot** to meet outside.

Joe holds the railing when he goes down the stairs. He does not run.

Leah skinned her knee. Mom gets the **first aid kit**. All better!

Safety Rules

- **Keep** small items **away** from younger kids.
- **Do not touch** the stovetop.
- **Follow** a fire safety plan.
- **Hold** the railing when walking down stairs.
- Be **prepared** with a first aid kit.

Glossary

accidents

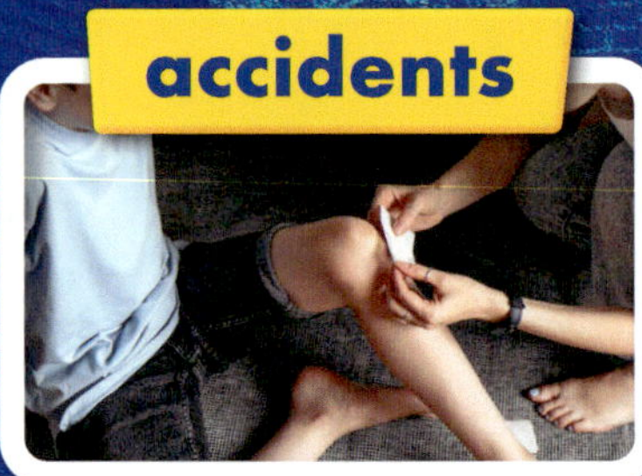

sudden events when someone is hurt

first aid kit

a bag or box with items to help people who are hurt or sick

prepared

ready to do something

risks

chances that something bad could happen

smoke alarm

an item that makes noise when it senses smoke

To Learn More

AT THE LIBRARY

Catena, Melissa. *Fire Safety*. Minneapolis, Minn.: Jump!, 2025.

Chang, Kirsten. *Street Safety*. Minneapolis, Minn.: Bellwether Media, 2027.

Owens, Layla. *I Stay Safe*. Buffalo, N.Y.: Enslow Publishing, 2026.

ON THE WEB

FACTSURFER

Factsurfer.com gives you a safe, fun way to find more information.

1. Go to www.factsurfer.com.
2. Enter "safety at home" into the search box and click 🔍.
3. Select your book cover to see a list of related content.

Index

The images in this book are reproduced through the courtesy of: RichVintage, front cover (top); ferrantraite/ Getty Images, front cover (bottom); manfredxy, p. 3 (alarm); Femke, p. 3 (kit); New Africa, pp. 4-5, 22 (first aid kit); Prostock-studio, pp. 6-7; dsheremeta, pp. 8-9; Pixel-Shot, pp. 10-11; FatCamera, pp. 12-13; SolStock, pp. 14-15; Anatoliy Karlyuk, pp. 16-17; Andrey Popov, p. 17 (inset); AzmanL, pp. 18-19; StockPlanets, p. 19 (inset); Zinkevych, pp. 20-21; Liliia Bila, p. 21 (inset); Anastasia Dobrusina, p. 22 (accidents); David Pereiras, p. 22 (prepared); Monkey Business, p. 22 (risks); fergregory, p. 22 (smoke alarm).